EFFECTIVE
RESUME WRITING
A GUIDE TO SUCCESSFUL EMPLOYMENT

NEAL PUBLICATIONS, INC.
127 West Indiana Avenue
P.O. Box 451
Perrysburg, Ohio 43551-0451 U.S.A.

Publishers of

Effective Phrases For Performance Appraisals
A Guide To Successful Evaluations
Effective Letters For Business, Professional and Personal Use
A Guide To Successful Correspondence
Your Slice Of The Melon
A Guide To Greater Job Success

EFFECTIVE
RESUME WRITING
A GUIDE TO SUCCESSFUL EMPLOYMENT

Neal Publications, Inc.
127 West Indiana Avenue
P.O. Box 451
Perrysburg, Ohio 43551-0451 U.S.A.

First Edition 1991

ISBN 0-9609006-8-3
SAN 240-8198
Library of Congress Catalog Card Number: 90-063084

FOREWORD

A resume is a presentation of your employment qualifications. A good resume is straight-forward and emphasizes your education, employment history and other qualifications.

Professional resumes are clear, concise and designed to stimulate interest. The content of a resume is largely determined by the career stage of the applicant. A student seeking a part-time job will require a resume which is basically a fact sheet. In contrast, a person in mid-career will require a two page resume with heavy emphasis on experience and accomplishments.

This publication contains basic guidelines for preparing an effective resume. It must be recognized that a standard resume simply does not exist for every person and situation. However, a number of sample resumes covering a variety of career situations are included to provide a basic reference.

Resumes are merely one element of the job search process. Transmittal letters and interviewing are also critical elements. The sample transmittal letters are designed to attract attention, convey a dynamic personal image and stimulate action. Examples of transmittal letters are included and suggestions for strengthening your interviewing skills are also discussed.

It is hoped that the material will greatly assist you in achieving your highest career objectives.

TABLE OF CONTENTS

I

Principles of a Powerful Resume

IMPORTANCE OF RESUMES

Increasing job mobility is creating a strong need for effective resume writing. Mergers, acquisitions and reorganizations have resulted in growing job insecurity for more and more employees. Corporations often give short notice of terminations providing strong justification for maintaining a powerful and current resume.

Career oriented individuals particularly in mature organizations need effective resumes for seeking positions offering greater responsibilities, challenges and rewards.

FORMAT

A standard format is not suitable for all persons. A chronological listing works well for most people. It merely lists employment history, education etc. in chronological order with the latest date appearing first. The chronological listing is especially suitable for persons without large gaps in their backgrounds. A chronological listing is easier to read and is considered to be the preferred format.

A skills oriented approach is desirable for persons who have weaknesses or large gaps in their backgrounds. When using a skills format, we recommend three or more broad categories such as the following:

Suggested Broad Skills Categories

administering	evaluating
budgeting	managing
communicating	organizing
controlling	planning
directing	supervising

Skills may also be listed in greater detail to meet the requirements of a specific position as follows:

Examples of Specific Skills Categories

compensating	recruiting
evaluating	screening
interviewing	testing
placing	training

The skills format is often viewed by professional personnel people as a means to camouflage shortcomings. We recommend the skills format for special situations only. In some situations, a combination of the chronological and skills formats is suitable.

CONTENTS

Resumes in the early career stage are short and simple. As your career grows, you will be able to concentrate on major accomplishments while deleting details that have become relatively insignificant.

A job seeker with a very strong academic background may find the inclusion of interests, community activities and athletic accomplishments to be totally unnecessary and may actually detract from the educational achievement.

Conversely, a person with a weak academic background may find it advisable to include interests, community activities and athletic achievements in order to place emphasis on personal skills.

Remember, your resume is competing with many others. You want to give the prospective employer reasons for hiring you. Your potential will be determined largely on the basis of what you have done in the past. You want your accomplishments to stand out as hard evidence of your past performance and serve as a springboard to greater success.

ACCURACY

A major requirement of effective resume writing is honesty. You need to accurately describe your strengths and accomplishments while embellishing them to the fullest degree. Everyone needs to put their best foot forward and you may be sure that competing resumes will include much puffery.

Today, many companies are taking extreme measures to avoid employment litigation. In response to inquiries on former employees, more and more firms are limiting their replies to a statement of employment history. Since you cannot rely on recommendations of former employers, you need to strongly emphasize your past accomplishments.

It is essential that you make every effort to use exact titles, employment dates, etc. For example, if you were a Territory Representative, don't state that you were a Territory Manager. Instead, state that as Territory Representative, you managed the territory. Accuracy is also critical when listing schools attended or degrees received.

While employers are prohibited from asking certain questions on application forms and during interviews, they can be very sophisticated in learning and verifying employment statements using a variety of sources. Credit reports, for example, provide a wealth of information on a candidate.

Organizations can be very sophisticated in verifying employment statements and total honesty will eliminate any concerns.

APPEARANCE

From a mechanical standpoint, you want your resume to look clean, clear and concise. Make your strongest statements stand out by placing them at the end of a paragraph where they will be surrounded by space. Avoid the appearance of a mass mailing. You should also avoid resumes with bright colors, unusual shapes etc. In some fields such as advertising, merchandising and creative services, unusual resumes are common and appropriate.

CONFIDENTIALITY

If you are currently employed, you should not hesitate to request that the resume be kept confidential. Although employers understand and respect the need for confidentiality, mentioning this point provides added assurance.

II

How Employers Will Handle Your Resume

It is important to understand what happens to your resume after it is received at a prospective employer. Some large firms receive hundreds of resumes a week. Each resume is usually scanned by a clerical person who is given specific guidelines for automatic rejection. Minimum requirements might include graduation from college and several years of related work experience. Rejections at this level are sent directly to the word processor for acknowledgement.

You want to be sure that your resume passes the first hurdle by meeting basic job requirements. If your resume varies slightly from specified requirements, it is best to omit the weak area.

Once a resume passes the initial scanning process, it is forwarded to the Personnel Manager. He or she will often spend less than a minute scanning the resume placing desirable candidates in a separate file. Eventually, the remaining resumes will be read in greater detail with sections often highlighted.

Interviews will be extended to the chosen candidates. After several applicants are interviewed, the personnel department will arrange for interviews with the department head who has the job opening. The hiring department will usually make the final selection from the candidates who have been pre-screened by the personnel department.

In short, the resume process at large organizations may be viewed as a large pyramid. Hundreds of resumes come in at the bottom but only a very few progress upward to the serious hiring level.

Efforts to directly contact the hiring department can be very productive. Although a department manager will be required under company policy to return your inquiry to the personnel department for formal processing, it takes just a little comment to get you in the running. For example, a department head may note on a follow-up letter regarding a telephone contact, "I talked to this person who sounds like an excellent candidate — believe we should look seriously at this one — HRB." Since the personnel department is in a staff capacity, they will usually conform to the wishes of a hiring manager.

The relationship between the personnel department and the various hiring departments must be handled delicately. Personnel people often have strong egos and believe they are the only persons capable of professionally handling job applicants. On the other hand, the hiring department must work with the chosen person and good chemistry between the immediate supervisor and the person hired is essential. Also, the cost center of the hiring department will absorb all payroll costs placing the supervisor in a strong decision-making position.

In smaller companies, resumes are usually sent to the Personnel Manager who rejects applicants that do not meet minimum standards. The remaining resumes are forwarded to the department manager who has the opening. The department head will review the resumes and advise the personnel department of the persons selected for interviews. The department head will interview the applicants and make the final decision.

III

Guidelines for a Winning Resume

GENERAL

- Be honest.

- Embellish, but do not exaggerate.

- Concentrate on your strengths and goals.

- Use powerful action verbs to describe accomplishments (created, initiated, developed, increased, trained etc.)

- Do not omit any education or employment history.

- Capitalize on the reputations of former employers. Many prospective employers are impressed with applicants who have previously worked for highly respected organizations. In every field, there are leading companies, medical centers, law firms, libraries, museums, universities etc. If you have been employed by a noted organization, make every effort to emphasize your previous employer's name.

- Do not be humorous.

- Avoid any references to religion or political activities.

- Write with enthusiasm.

- Check each word to ensure correct spelling.

- Prepare a draft and review it the next day.

- Ask trusted friends to review and comment on your resume.

APPEARANCE

- Use top quality 24 lb. or more paper, preferably ivory, white or grey.

- If possible, have your resume typed on a computer and printed on a laser printer. Many universities and copy shops have computers and printers available for this use.

- Do not use brilliant colored paper or unusual shapes and designs.

- It is not necessary to type "Resume" above your name.

- Prepare a balanced format allowing for sufficient blank space.

- Make strong statements stand out by surrounding them with space.

- Use bold type to highlight headings.

- Never exceed two pages.

- If your resume is two pages, place a staple on an angle at the top left and make sure your name is on the second page.

CAREER OBJECTIVE

The career objective statement is a critical element of your resume. You should state your career objective regardless of whether you are applying for a part-time, temporary or full-time position. Be sure your career objective is realistic.

When preparing your career objective, you need to consider your current position and your career ambitions. If you are applying for entry level positions, your career objective should be broad and may not even emphasize your major field of study. However, if you have had several years experience in one field and you know exactly the type of position you are willing to accept, your career objective will likely be more specific.

It is important to recognize that your greatest potential is usually in the area where you already excel. For example, the author has seen a large number of star sales persons fail miserably in positions of sales management. If you are an outstanding office supply sales person, you might have more going for you by accepting a higher level position selling computers rather than a sales manager of office supplies.

The same situation is often seen in the administrative area. Executive secretaries frequently desire to leave the field for more prestigious positions in administrative management. However, an outstanding executive secretary in search of greater responsibility may have more to offer in the marketplace by seeking a similar position working for a higher ranking executive at a larger firm.

SUGGESTED CAREER OBJECTIVES

Below are some sample career objectives that you may wish to use in your resume.

- I am seeking an entry level position which will offer opportunities for career growth in the field of *accounting*.

- I am seeking a challenging position offering greater responsibility.

- I am seeking a position where my skills in *advertising, merchandising* and *public relations* will be fully utilized and challenged.

- I am seeking a challenging position in *elementary teaching* where I can fully apply my education and experiences.

- I wish to obtain a position as a *computer programmer* which will lead to greater responsibilities in management information services.

- I desire a position in *nursing* which will provide strong advancement opportunities.

- To manage the advertising department of a medium size firm with full responsibility for *creativity, programming* and *agency selection*.

- To be an *executive secretary* with key management responsibilities.

- To be a *personnel supervisor* specializing in *recruiting, placement* and *training* of personnel.

14

SIGNIFICANT ACCOMPLISHMENTS

Whenever possible, describe accomplishments in quantitative terms such as increased sales by 12% between 19___ and 19___ . . . increased annual production by 7% compared to the prior year . . . reduced the number of defects by approximately 4% between 19___ and 19___.

Be careful not to exaggerate when describing your accomplishments. Adding the words "about" or "approximately" may actually give increased credibility. Keep in mind that organizations are looking for team players. Whenever the opportunity arises, indicate that you and your department, project team, etc. were able to reach specific goals.

Include any accomplishments that relate to special employer programs. For example, "As Chairman of the Company's Red Cross Blood Donation Drive, I was able to increase donations by 9%." Similarly "As a member of the Company's Executive Loan Program, I was successful in helping to achieve a 4% increase in 19___ United Appeal corporate pledges."

If your accomplishments do not lend themselves to complete sentences, use bullets separated by three dots. For example: . . . increased the number of widget distributors in my district by 20% between 19___ and 19___ . . . created a district widget program which was expanded nationally . . . achieved record sales in my district for 19___ and 19___. If bullets are used, be sure to make complete and understandable statements.

EMPLOYMENT HISTORY

- List most recent employment first.

- State city and state of former employers.

- Do not state the actual names of former supervisors.

- Indicate if position was full or part-time (early career stage only).

- Indicate job title, responsibilities and specific accomplishments.

- Decrease the detail as work experience increases.

- Avoid gaps in employment history.

- If you are returning to the work force, emphasize any volunteer work or community service.

15

EDUCATION

- List most recent school first.

- If you have attended college, state the name of any degree earned and the name, city and state of all colleges attended.

- If you have earned a four year college degree, do not list any high schools attended more than five years ago unless you were in top 25% of class.

- State degrees being sought.

- If applying for entry level positions:
  — State grade average if 3.0 or higher on a 4.0
  — State class rank if in the top third
  — State all memberships, offices held and other school activities (except political or religious)

- Include any seminars or workshops you have attended whenever a seminar relates to the position being sought. State the subject such as "Just-In-Time Inventory Management" — National Management Association — 19__.

HOBBIES AND INTERESTS

It is generally not recommended that you include hobbies and interests unless they relate to the position which you are seeking. For example, you would include photography if you were applying for a position as a newspaper copywriter or editor.

MEMBERSHIPS

List only associations or organizations that are career related. Avoid listing any organizations that are controversial.

MILITARY SERVICE

State military service in order to avoid gaps in your background. List rank whenever progression is indicated. Describe military experience in civilian terms as much as possible.

PERSONAL

We do not recommend that you include personal information such as age, height, weight, etc. The inclusion of personal data is a no win situation. Someone can always find fault and the disadvantages far outweigh any advantages.

SALARY

Do not list any reference to salary on your resume. You do not want to provide any information which could cause your automatic rejection at the clerical level.

If you are applying for an entry level position, it is especially critical that you avoid any reference to salary. You do not want to commit yourself to a specific salary or range which may change depending on the circumstances. If the position is ideal and offers fast advancement opportunities, you may be willing to accept a lower salary.

Employers will often request salary information in an advertisement or on the formal application form. While you need to provide accurate information on previous salaries, we recommend that you respond to all future salary inquiries with the statement "to be negotiated." Recognize that fringe benefits vary widely among employers and may represent 40% of your salary. You are not in a position to state salary requirements until you know all the facts.

If you are an experienced professional and know your market value, you may wish to provide a broad salary range. However, always stress that you are open to negotiation. By following this approach, employers will not waste your time interviewing you for a position which they cannot come close to paying your minimum requirements. Since job titles may not always reflect the salary (a Project Director at one company can make $20,000 and at another $100,000), it can be most frustrating to have several interviews at an organization only to find out that their salary range is far below what you are willing to accept.

If you decide to send a salary history, the following example will be helpful. It should be sent along with the transmittal letter and resume.

John W. Smith
Salary History

Project Director — ABC Company
19__ to 19__
Annual Base Salary: $35,000
End of Year Bonus: $9,000
Total: $44,000

Assistant Research Director — ABC Company
19__ to 19__
Annual Base Salary: $30,000
End of Year Bonus: $10,500
Total: $40,500

Senior Research Analyst — XYZ Company
19__ to 19__
Annual Base Salary: $25,000

PHOTOGRAPHS

It is generally not recommended that you provide your photograph. Companies are very conscious of potential discrimination charges and they may not wish to file any material that could serve as possible evidence.

Additionally, photographs are always taken under ideal conditions. You do not want to create a situation where the interviewer may feel that your appearance does not convey the high expectations of your photograph.

Photographs are obviously necessary when submitting portfolios for positions such as television reporting, modeling etc. In other special situations, a professionally taken color photo should be glued to the top right corner on the front page. Be sure to write your name on the back of the photo.

REASON FOR LEAVING

Do not list any reason for leaving a former employer. If requested on an application form, the reason should always be positive. For example, "sought a position where I could better apply my education and experience."

REFERENCES

- Never give a prospective employer references until they ask.

- Do not list actual names of references on your resume.

- Consider using former supervisors or associates who are retired or no longer work for your former employers. Persons who have left organizations can be very supportive in your job hunting efforts.

- Do not use relatives or members of the clergy as references.

- References should know your work and/or academic abilities.

- Obtain prior approval before giving a person's name as a reference.

- Advise your former and current landlords and neighbors that you are applying for a job and they may be contacted for information.

- Prepare a typed sheet of the names, addresses and phone numbers of at least three references.

ACTION ORIENTED

Make your resume appear lively by placing heavy emphasis on action verbs. Take credit for your accomplishments and convey the image that you are a leader who gets things done.

The following action verbs will help you.

ACTION VERBS

accelerated	adapted	applied
accentuated	addressed	appointed
accepted	adhered	appraised
accomplished	adjusted	appropriated
accounted	administered	approved
achieved	adopted	arranged
acquainted	advanced	articulated
acquired	advised	ascended
acted	allocated	ascertained
activated	analyzed	assembled
actuated	anticipated	asserted

assessed	consummated	encouraged
assigned	contemplated	enforced
assimilated	continued	engineered
assisted	contributed	enhanced
assumed	controlled	enlightened
assured	converted	enriched
attained	conveyed	ensured
attended	cooperated	established
audited	coordinated	estimated
augmented	corrected	evaluated
authorized	created	evoked
averted	cultivated	examined
avoided	decentralized	exceeded
broadened	decreased	excelled
built	dedicated	executed
calculated	defined	exercised
capitalized	delegated	exhibited
centralized	delivered	expanded
challenged	demonstrated	expected
checked	designated	expedited
circulated	designed	explored
clarified	determined	expressed
cleared	developed	extended
coached	devised	extracted
collaborated	devoted	facilitated
collected	directed	financed
combined	discharged	focused
commanded	discovered	forecasted
communicated	displayed	formed
compiled	disseminated	formulated
completed	distinguished	fostered
complied	distributed	founded
composed	documented	fulfilled
comprehended	doubled	furnished
computed	drafted	gained
conceived	earned	generated
concentrated	edited	guided
concluded	effected	handled
condensed	elicited	headed
conducted	eliminated	helped
conformed	emphasized	hired
conjected	employed	identified
considered	empowered	implemented
consolidated	emulated	impressed
consulted	encompassed	improved

improvised
increased
influenced
informed
initiated
inspected
inspired
installed
instigated
instituted
instructed
integrated
interpreted
interviewed
introduced
invented
invested
investigated
issued
launched
lectured
led
lightened
liquidated
located
made
maintained
managed
marketed
mediated
minimized
mobilized
modernized
modified
monitored
motivated
necessitated
negotiated
notified
observed
obtained
operated
optimized
orchestrated
ordered

organized
originated
overcame
overhauled
oversaw
paced
participated
performed
perpetuated
pinpointed
pioneered
planned
possessed
practiced
prepared
presented
prevented
processed
procured
produced
programmed
projected
promoted
proposed
proved
provided
published
purchased
pursued
realized
received
recognized
recommended
reconciled
recorded
recruited
redesigned
reduced
re-established
reflected
regulated
reinforced
rejected
related
released

renegotiated
reorganized
reported
represented
required
researched
reshaped
resolved
respected
responded
restored
revamped
reviewed
revised
revitalized
revived
saved
scheduled
secured
seeked
selected
served
set up
settled
shared
showed
simplified
sold
solved
sorted
sparked
specified
sponsored
staffed
standardized
started
stimulated
streamlined
strengthened
stretched
structured
studied
submitted
suggested
summarized

supervised	trained	used
supported	transacted	utilized
surpassed	transferred	verified
surveyed	transformed	vitalized
sustained	translated	weighted
tailored	treated	widened
taught	trimmed	won
terminated	tripled	worked
tested	uncovered	wrote
tightened	undertook	
traded	unified	

IV

Self-Examination Checklist

Before you begin to write your resume, you need to examine yourself. Plan to concentrate on your strengths and avoid your weaknesses.

The following checklist will stimulate your thinking and provide the information needed to effectively prepare your resume.

SELF-EXAMINATION CHECKLIST
Student

Did you excel in any subjects?

Do you have a high overall grade average?

Did you receive any honors or recognitions?

Did you display leadership skills in athletics?

Were you a class officer?

Were you a club officer?

Did you serve on any student committees?

Were you a cheerleader or member of the band?

Were you a member of the yearbook staff?

Did you volunteer for any charitable organizations?

Were you a camp counselor, coach etc?

Did you participate in any job shadowing programs?

Did you participate in any internship programs?

SELF-EXAMINATION CHECKLIST
Career Person

COMMUNICATING

Did you speak before any conventions or organizations?

Did you present any technical papers?

Did you write any speeches, reports or manuals?

Have you had any articles published?

DEVELOPMENT

Did you participate in any management development programs?

Were you asked to attend seminars, workshops etc.?

Were your performance appraisals superior?

Did you train anyone?

EDUCATION

Have you received any special academic or other recognitions?

Did you attend a school where you can emphasize its reputation in a specific field?

Were you active in any extra-curriculum activities?

FINANCIAL

Did you devise or improve any financial controls?

Did you conform to budget?

Did you prepare any organization plans such as business plans, marketing plans etc.?

Did you make a specific contribution to increased profits?

MANAGEMENT

How many persons did you supervise?

Did you reorganize or implement new methods or procedures for greater efficiency?

Did you sell or acquire any companies, divisions, branches or outlets?

Did you improve earnings by a specific percent?

MANUFACTURING

Did you increase production by a specific percent?

Did you improve product quality by a specific percent?

Did you improve efficiency by a specific percent?

Did you purchase or install new machinery for greater efficiency?

MARKETING

Did you increase sales by a specific percent?

Did you increase market share by a specific percent?

Did you obtain any large or new accounts?

Did you successfully introduce any new products?

Did you improve the quality of service to customers, patients or clients?

Did you travel extensively?

MEDICINE

Did you initiate or make any improvements in patient care?

Did you improve administrative efficiency?

Were you involved in any research or experimental projects?

Are you specially trained in any area?

Do you hold any licenses or certifications?

MILITARY

What area of experience is most applicable to civilian life?

Did you receive any honors, awards or other special recognizations?

Did you travel extensively?

PROFESSIONAL ACTIVITIES AND RECOGNITIONS

Were you active in trade associations or professional organizations?

Did you serve on any advisory boards?

Were you on any selection committees?

Did you receive any awards or recognitions?

RESEARCH

Did you prepare or initiate any research or survey projects?

Did you invent or develop any products, processes or formulas?

Did you obtain any patents?

SELF-EXAMINATION CHECKLIST
Person Returning to Work Force

Have you maintained any memberships to keep abreast of your field?

Have you attended any classes or refresher courses in your field?

Have you kept informed of your field by reading the professional literature?

Have you maintained any licenses or certifications?

SELF-EXAMINATION CHECKLIST
Special Skills

Are you proficient in a foreign language?

Are you strong in computer skills?

Are you proficient in drawing or sketching?

Are you a skilled photographer?

Are you a good speaker or presenter?

Are you good at writing?

V

Flexible Resumes

Many persons have broad experience which provides opportunities for emphasizing strengths in selected areas to meet the requirements of various openings.

In the marketing area, for example, a Director of Advertising/Merchandising may also have responsibility for public relations. Resumes may be prepared to reflect sound backgrounds in advertising, merchandising or public relations.

With a word processor, resumes may be structured for instant deletions, insertions and other revisions. The three key areas that normally need to be revised are career objective, employment history and significant accomplishments. Spacing and balance are critical because the resume should not appear to be altered.

Flexible resumes are ideal for persons who are using a shot gun approach to job hunting.

VI

Special Problems

Following are some common problems that you can overcome when writing resumes.

Problem	Recommendation
Young — no experience	Emphasize education, ambitions and goals
Elderly	Emphasize experience, reliability and judgment
Many different jobs	Emphasize broad and diversified experience
Limited education	Stress practical, down-to-earth experience
Educational degree not in same field as job	Do not define degrees — for example, state B.B.A. rather than Bachelor of Business Administration. Also, emphasize well rounded education and broad thinking capabilites
Gaps in resume	Stress some type of compensating activity such as consulting, volunteer work or educational travel

VII

Resume Maintenance

Forcing yourself to maintain a current resume is a solid investment in your future.

Growing job insecurity is making employability your greatest personal strength. The increasing number of organizational restructurings are forcing more and more persons to begin unexpected job searches. You can anticipate a number of job changes during a career.

Since experience becomes more critical as you advance, it is essential that you maintain an accurate resume. The key is to keep a file of all new responsibilities and accomplishments. Many persons have stronger backgrounds than they realize.

Keep copies of job descriptions, organization charts and performance appraisals. You should also file any complimentary letters or memos. If compliments are not placed in writing, make a note such as "today Mr. Johnson, V-P Marketing, congratulated me on my contribution to the annual marketing plan."

Functions which may seem insignificant at the time, may later be used to establish a pattern of progression in a particular field.

VIII

Job Hunting Tips

The best source for finding a suitable job is personal acquaintances. More people obtain jobs through networking than any other means. You will want to contact friends, relatives, neighbors and anyone who can possibly provide you with leads. There is simply no substitute for personal referrals.

In cases where your employer is aware that you are seeking another job, do not overlook suppliers to your present firm. The author has seen many individuals obtain jobs with suppliers. Employers will often recommend an employee to a supplier and this can carry much clout. Employers seem comfortable knowing that a trusted former employee is working for a major supplier.

Mailing resumes in response to newspaper advertisements is one of the more common ways of seeking employment. Even if you do not meet all the requirements listed, it can do no harm to send a resume. Sometimes the company may have other openings where your skills are more suited.

Ads that give a company name are considered to offer better odds than a blind ad with only a P.O. box number. It is possible for some employers to test the waters by advertising jobs merely to see the caliber of applicants that can be attracted at a stated salary.

Sending resumes to organizations with unadvertised positions is not discouraged, however, it should be done with the knowledge that the odds are relatively low. If you do send unsolicited resumes, it is best to send them early in the year. Most companies restructure in October and November. Hirings begin in January when new budgets are in place and the coming year is filled with optimism.

Unsolicited resumes should be sent to all new organizations as well as those who are expanding. A job seeking person will want to keep a sharp eye out for magazine and newspaper articles announcing organizational developments and plans. Real estate articles often give advance notice of new plants, warehouses, additions, etc.

The journals and publications that trade associations and professional organizations publish can be another source for finding employment. College libraries will have journals related to your field and job advertisements can often be found in these publications. Some associations provide newsletters and job hotline numbers which give information on career opportunities.

Large organizations will sometimes provide job hotline numbers as well. At some personnel offices, lists of job openings are available for job hunters.

It is important not to overlook contacts with college placement offices and alumni associations. College placement offices can provide job listings, resume writing seminars, practice interviewing workshops and career counseling to persons who are entering the work force as well as those who have several years of experience. Alumni associations may sponsor job fairs and provide listings of employment opportunities. Some alumni magazines include special sections for alumni to advertise their job skills to other readers.

Executive search firms (also known as professional recruiters or headhunters) are another source that can be used to obtain employment. These firms first interview you, then arrange for interviews with companies that have positions open where your skills are needed. If you are hired, most firms receive a fee from the employer (stay away from firms which require you to pay the fee). Frequently, executive search firms specialize in a few specific fields, so make sure you contact the firms which can provide you with opportunities in your chosen area.

If using professional recruitment firms, be sure that you are being sent to prospective employers where you have a reasonable chance of obtaining a position. Some firms can forward a number of unqualified applicants to an employer for the purpose of making other and more qualified referrals look better.

You should explore every opportunity in your job seeking efforts. Nevertheless, personal contacts are likely to provide the biggest payoff.

IX

Transmittal Letters

The transmittal letter (also known as a cover letter) is a very critical element of your job search. Resumes are often similar in content, but the transmittal letter offers an opportunity to distinguish yourself. If responding to an advertisement, the transmittal letter can reiterate your strengths for a particular position.

At higher levels of management, a letter often replaces a resume. Likewise, a retiree seeking a part-time position may find a simple letter sufficient.

It is important that you keep accurate records of your job hunting activities. You will find it helpful to chart the dates of all transmittal letters.

TRANSMITTAL LETTER GUIDELINES

- Use high quality personal stationery that matches your resume paper.

- Keep the letter short and positive.

- Include your phone number(s).

- Request an interview and let them know you will be contacting them on a certain day.

- Mention any person who is both an acquaintance and employee of the prospective employer.

- If the letter is unsolicited, mail it to a person rather than a department. A name can be obtained by simply calling the company and asking for the name of the Director of Marketing, Director of Research, etc. Be sure to get an exact title.

- If you are currently employed, it is suggested that you state "Your keeping this inquiry confidential will be appreciated."

- Do not use first names in an effort to seek clearance past secretaries.

- Do not staple the letter to the resume.

- Mail the resume to arrive on Tuesday.

SAMPLE TRANSMITTAL LETTERS

Blind Inquiry/Unsolicited Letter

Dear _____:

    I am interested in seeking employment at _____. I believe my qualifications and experiences in _____, _____ and _____ would make a strong addition to your Company. A complete resume is enclosed.

    If any positions are available which could utilize my skills, I would appreciate an interview to discuss my potential contribution to your organization.

    Your keeping this inquiry confidential will be appreciated.

              Sincerely,

Blind Inquiry/Unsolicited Letter

Dear _____ :

I wish to apply for the position of _____ or a similar position in your Company.

I am presently a senior at _____ University majoring in _____. I will graduate this coming June with a degree in _____.

My goal is to pursue a career in _____. I am a conscientious, hard working person and believe that I could make a strong contribution to your organization. A resume is enclosed.

Your providing me with the opportunity of an interview would be greatly appreciated.

Sincerely,

Newspaper Advertisement

Dear _____ :

I am writing in response to the advertisement for the position of _____ which appeared in the _____ on _____.

I feel my degree in _____ and my experiences and qualifications in _____, _____ and _____ closely parallel the requirements outlined in your job listing. A resume is enclosed which details my education and work experiences.

I would very much appreciate an interview with you to further discuss my qualifications and potential contribution to your organization.

Sincerely,

Newspaper Advertisement

I am writing in response to your employment advertisement which appeared in the (date) edition of the (name of paper).

I feel confident that you would be interested in a person who offers:

A strong education with a degree in _____.

The ability to draw on all available resources to meet goals, objectives and deadlines.

An enthusiastic attitude combined with the ability to work well with others.

Since I possess these abilities, I wish to apply for your opening.

I will call you next (day) regarding an interview to personally discuss my strengths with you.

Sincerely,

Newspaper Advertisement

Dear _____:

I read with much interest your employment ad in the (month, day) edition of the _____.

Since my education and experience would be ideally suited for the position of _____, I wish to apply.

I am a graduate of _____ with a degree in _____. For the past two years, I have been employed by a leading manufacture of _____. As _____, my duties currently include responsibility for _____, _____ and _____. Enclosed is a complete resume.

I would welcome an opportunity to personally discuss my qualifications with you.

Your keeping this inquiry confidential will be appreciated.

Sincerely,

Newspaper Advertisement

Dear _____ :

I read with much interest your advertisement in the (day) issue of _____ .

I feel confident that you would be interested in an individual who offers:

Solid experience in _____

A strong supervisory background

Enthusiasm, initiative and dedication

If you are looking for an individual with these traits, please refer to my enclosed resume.

Your arranging an interview with me would be greatly appreciated. I will call you next (day) morning and look forward to discussing my qualifications.

Sincerely,

Loss of a job due to restructuring — Senior management

Dear _____ :

As you may know, ABC company was recently acquired by XYZ Company. Following the takeover, many management employees of ABC, including myself, were released.

I served _____ years with the Company and most recently held the position of Manager, Sales Promotion. My major responsibilities included sales promotion in support of our marketing objectives for the _____ product line. I was responsible for a 3 million dollar annual budget. My campaigns were a major factor contributing to the 14% sales increase last year on the line.

Additionally, I managed the corporate co-op program for the Company and its 750 wholesalers. I was responsible for introducing a new auditing system which reduced duplicate co-op costs last year by 11%. A complete resume is enclosed.

I would welcome an opportunity to discuss my qualifications with you. I will call you next (day) morning and look forward to talking with you.

Sincerely,

Referral

Dear _____ :

A friend of mine, Mr. _____ of your firm, has suggested that I apply for the position of _____.

I have always admired your Company and believe that I could make a substantial contribution to your continued success. Enclosed is my resume.

I will call your office next (<u>day</u>) morning and would very much appreciate the courtesy of an interview.

        Sincerely,

Summer Job

Dear _____ :

I wish to apply for a summer position at _____.

I am a responsible person and enjoy working with the public. As a sophomore at _____, I am maintaining a 3.2 grade average on a 4 point scale. Enclosed is a resume.

Your providing me with an opportunity to personally discuss my qualifications would be greatly appreciated.

        Sincerely,

X

Resume Follow-Up

One of the most frustrating experiences of job hunting is to forward a resume and receive no response whatsoever. Most large firms will send an acknowledgement stating that (1) your qualifications do not match the requirements of the current opening or (2) your application continues to be under consideration or (3) the position has been filled. Smaller companies often do not acknowledge the receipt of resumes.

Additionally, the bureaucracy of many organizations makes the hiring process a lengthy one. Companies want to cover themselves from many angles which adds to employment delays.

If you do not receive an acknowledgement after three weeks including mailing time, we recommend that you send a follow-up letter. You do not want to harrass the prospective employer but you certainly are entitled to know whether they received the resume and are being considered.

A follow-up letter may actually work to your advantage because it will help keep your file active and demonstrate that you are a conscientious and serious-minded individual. Telephone calls are not recommended because your inquiry is too likely to be handled by a person who lacks authority.

It is reasonable to send follow-up letters only to the prospective employers where you believe that your chances are especially good. If you send out two hundred resumes, selective follow-up is obviously more critical.

SUGGESTED RESUME FOLLOW-UP LETTER

Mr. Robert G. Jones
Vice President Sales
ABC Corporation
One Presidential Drive
Anytown, USA

Dear Mr. Jones:

On (<u>name</u> <u>of</u> <u>day, month</u> <u>date</u>), I forwarded a resume in response to your add in the (<u>month day</u>) edition of the _____. As of today, I have not received a reply.

I continue to be very interested in the position of _____. I am enclosing another resume in case you did not receive the previous copy.

Any information that you could forward concerning the status of my application would be greatly appreciated.

Sincerely,

XI

Successful Interviewing

Prepare yourself for an interview by learning as much as possible about the prospective employer.

If the employer is a national firm, visit a large library to read about the company. Be sure to study the annual report which can sometimes be found at major libraries. You can also obtain annual reports by calling the public relations department of the firm. We strongly recommend that you read reports of the company prepared by the stock advisory services. Most large libraries subscribe to the major investment newsletters which often provide excellent insight on firms. Some large libraries also offer computerized information retrieval systems.

You can favorably impress employers by doing some field research. For example, a person applying for a position with a major paint manufacturer would find it advisable to visit stores who handle the product line. By talking to store personnel, you can learn about any new products, promotions or other current developments. Make every effort to uncover positive information.

During the interview, you can casually say that "your marketers are certainly enthusiastic about your new ABC line. I understand from talking with several of your dealers that the product is selling so fast they can hardly keep the exterior white in stock!"

Comments of this type will demonstrate that you are a resourceful and conscientious person. While this type of approach is certain to impress personnel people, you can imagine how it will really hit a button with marketing executives!

Group interviewing is becoming more common especially in second interviews. It is important that you know the positions of the persons who will be jointly interviewing you. Obviously, you want to make statements that will impress each member of the interviewing committee.

For example, assume you are interviewing for the position of Assistant Manager of Marketing Research. You have previously learned that the interviewing committee will consist of the Manager of Marketing Research, Sales Manager and Manager of Accounting.

You will need to impress the Manager of Marketing Research by demonstrating that you are proficient in developing questionnaires, conducting focus groups and analyzing statistics. You can impress the Sales Manager by stating that you believe the basic purpose of marketing research is to provide information that will support the sales group in achieving higher objectives. The Manager of Accounting can be impressed by pointing out that you always use the lowest statistically valid sample in order to achieve maximum cost efficiency.

Plan to arrive approximately ten minutes before the scheduled interview.

Keep in mind that the most critical part of the interview is the first several minutes. Interviewers tend to make their decisions early in the interview. Obviously, positive first impressions are vital.

Plan to begin with small talk. Know the current sport standings, the weather outlook and any late breaking news.

Be prepared to answer the following questions:

Questions to Anticipate in an Interview

Tell me a little about yourself.

Why do you feel that you are qualified for the job?

What are your strengths?

What are your weaknesses?

What is your greatest accomplishment?

Why do you want this position?

Describe how you would handle or have handled a confrontation with a (customer, client, parent etc.)

Where do you see yourself five or ten years from now?

Why should I hire you?

Are you willing to relocate?

Since the interview is a two-way street, you should also ask some questions to establish the seriousness of your career pursuit. Suggested questions are:

Questions To Ask In An Interview

Why is the position open?

What are the short and long range plans of your firm?

What career paths would be available to me?

Does the organization provide management development or educational support programs?

How often does your firm formally evaluate employee performance?

If possible, let the interviewer talk approximately 60-70% of the time. The interviewer is unlikely to be critical of the interview if he or she dominates it.

If the interviewer probes into one of your weak areas, be prepared to go on the offensive. For example, "I am glad you asked that question. I took five years to complete college because I had to spend one year working full-time to save enough money to continue my education."

Do not say anything negative about former employers or superiors.

Never get into a defensive position.

Other Interviewing Tips

Dress conservatively with blue and white the preferred colors.

Maintain eye contact with the interviewer.

Do not smoke.

When departing, thank the interviewer by repeating his or her name aloud and state that you hope to hear favorably.

Shake hands firmly.

POST INTERVIEW LETTER

Dear _____ :

Thank you for the interview on <u>day, month</u>.

I was certainly impressed with your fine facilities and knowledgeable personnel.

I feel quite confident that I can excel in the position of _____. Please continue to give my application every consideration.

Your interest is very much appreciated and I am looking forward to hearing from you.

Sincerely,

POST INTERVIEW LETTER

Dear ————— :

I wish to thank you for my interview on (<u>day, month</u>).

After learning more about your (<u>company, school, hospital etc.</u>), I am confident that I can make an important contribution to your organization.

If you require any additional information concerning my qualifications, please let me know. I can be reached at —————.

I certainly appreciate the many courtesies extended to me and hope to hear favorably from you.

Sincerely,

POST INTERVIEW LETTER

I just want to thank you for the interview on (<u>month day</u>).

I really enjoyed talking to you and learning more about your fine organization.

Your current opening continues to be of great interest to me. I feel confident that I could excel in the position and make an important contribution to your Company.

Your giving me every consideration will be very much appreciated.

Sincerely,

XII

Keeping a Positive Mental Outlook

The best time to look for a new position is when you already have one. Unfortunately, more and more terminations are occurring with no advance notice.

Following a termination, you are likely to feel depressed. A feeling of worthlessness and hurt is natural and understandable. You simply cannot let emotions control your destiny. The only response to a sudden termination is action.

Since you cannot devote all of your time to job hunting, you need to keep your life in balance as much as possible. Exercise, good eating and sleeping habits are essential.

You can help pass free time by reading or getting actively involved in a new activity. Persons at certain levels may be able to do some consulting. Other individuals may find it possible to teach an evening course at a local university or community college. You may find it beneficial to take a class in a special subject. Volunteer work is always another option.

The goal is to keep busy, maintain your self-esteem and build your spirits. As time passes, you will find it much easier to tell a prospective employer that you have been improving your qualifications by taking a computer course rather than just waiting around for the mail to arrive.

Many persons have endured sudden terminations and you can too. Individuals often look back at terminations and feel that it was one of the best things that ever happened to them. Terminations can be the catalyst that propels your career to new heights.

Keep your thoughts positive and direct all your energies to achieving greater success. The mere fact that you are reading this paragraph indicates that you are self-reliant and motivated.

Look upon your current situation as a golden opportunity to better yourself. This episode in your life will pass and you can make it one of your most rewarding experiences.

XIII

Sample Resumes

Chronological Format

SAMPLE RESUME
Senior Marketing

WILLIAM R. DOE
Street
City, State
(000) 000-0000

Career Objective

To achieve a Vice-President of Marketing position offering greater responsibility at the senior management level.

Employment History

19-- to present

Vice-President of Marketing, XYZ Manufacturing Corporation, City, State
Presently responsible for all marketing activities including advertising, distribution, marketing research, merchandising, public relations and sales. Plan, develop and implement corporate marketing strategies to ensure continued growth.

19-- to 19--

Director of Marketing, DEF Company, City, State
Directed all marketing functions with heavy emphasis on the development of new products. Responsible for a $45 million annual budget including a 100 person sales force selling to over 1500 distributor accounts.

19-- to 19--

Sales Manager, ABC Company, City, State
Managed a 75 person sales force selling a broad line of ignition parts to automotive parts wholesalers. Supervised three Regional Sales Managers.

19-- to 19--

District Sales Manager, Widget Manufacturing, Inc., City, State
Called on automotive jobbers and retailers selling ignition parts. Implemented all advertising, merchandising and sales programs.

Education

19-- to 19--

University of America, City, State, B.B.A. with a major in marketing

19--

"Success Selling" — Seminar, National Association of Sales Executives. "Planning Marketing Strategy" — Seminar, University of the South

Significant Accomplishments

Successfully introduced new line of electronic ignition products which generated $38 million in additional sales during the first year and provided a 7% increase in profit.

References

The best of references will be furnished upon request.

Functional Format

SAMPLE RESUME
Senior Marketing

William R. Doe
Street
City, State, Zip
(000) 000-0000

Career Objective

To achieve a Vice-President of Marketing position offering greater responsibility at the senior management level.

Experience

Budgeting — Responsible for a $45 million annual budget incorporating high profit objectives and strong variance control.

Managing — Managed all marketing activities including advertising, distribution, marketing research, merchandising, public relations and sales.

Planning — Planned, developed and implemented corporate marketing strategies to ensure continued growth.

Selling — Sold automotive parts to distributors, jobbers, retailers and national accounts.

Employment History

19-- to 19-- — Vice-President of Marketing, XYZ Manufacturing Corporation, City, State

19-- to 19-- — Director of Marketing, DEF Company, City, State

19-- to 19-- — Sales Manager, ABC Company, City, State

19-- to 19-- — District Sales Manager, Widget Manufacturing, Incorporated, City, State

Education

19-- to 19-- — University of America, City, State, B.B.A. with a major in marketing

19-- — "Success Selling" — Seminar, National Association of Sales Executives.

19-- — "Planning Marketing Strategy" — Seminar, University of the South

**Significant
Accomplishments**   Successfully introduced new line of electronic ignition products which generated $38 million in additional sales during the first year and provided a 7% increase in profit.

References   The best of references will be furnished upon request.

SAMPLE RESUME
Advertising

ROBERT L. DOE

Street
City, State, ZIP
(000) 000-0000

PROFESSIONAL OBJECTIVE

I am seeking a growth position where I can fully utilize my education and background in advertising production.

EDUCATION

19___ thru 19___	University Of The West
	City, State
	Bachelor of Fine Arts
	Major: Graphic Design
	Minor: Photography and Offset Printing
	Activities: Production Advertising Manager for School Newspaper
	Advertising Club – Vice-President

EMPLOYMENT

19___ thru 19___	West Coast Publications, Inc.
	City, State
	Production Artist
	Produced artwork for magazine advertisements and catalogs.

19___ thru 19___	Mid California University
	City, State
	Instructor
	Taught Commercial Avertising Photography

19___ thru 19___	William B. Doe Photography, Inc.
	City, State
	Studio Manager/Darkroom Technician/Photographer
	Photographed merchandise for major catalog retailer including _____, _____ and _____. Processed film and prepared for presentation to retail executives.

19___ thru 19___	Free-lance Photographer
	Provided full photographic services for advertisements, book covers, brochures, magazines, newspapers and other commercial purposes

SPECIAL STRENGTHS

Excel in advertising layout, art direction, four stat camera and spec type.

REFERENCES

References and portfolio will be furnished upon request.

SAMPLE RESUME
Engineering-Civil

Roger M. Doe
Street
City, State, Zip
(000) 000-0000

Professional Objective

To achieve a management position in civil engineering where I can fully apply my professional strengths.

Employment History

19-- to present: Engineering Supervisor, Smith, Jones and Wilson, Inc., City, State. Supervise five staff structural engineers in planning and designing rural bridges, approaches and tunnels. Prepare schematics for projects over $1 million. Coordinate all non-technical factors such as legal, social, economic and asthetic.

19-- to 19--: Structural Engineer, Newman Construction and Design, Inc. City, State. Prepared design plans for projects under $500,000. Supervised three engineering technicians who monitored construction sites for adherence to plans and designs. Coordinated all costs with contractors, state and local agencies. Prepared cost estimates for sales management.

Education

19-- to 19--: University of the East, City, State, B.S. with a major in civil engineering.

19--: "Current Developments In Civil Engineering" — Seminar, National Association of Civil Engineers.

19--: "Environmental Concerns For Civil Engineering" — Seminar, Environment Protection Agency — 19--.

Significant Accomplishments

Discovered a design weakness resulting from insufficient boring tests which saved $1 million in planned design costs. Planned a drainage system surrounding a four lane bridge which diverted polluted water to a sanitary system resulting in a $500,000 cost savings. Designed a bridge for Rolling Hills Country Club of City, State which won the 19-- award for Excellence In Design by the American Society of Civil Engineers.

Professional Organizations

American Society of Civil Engineers, State Engineering Society

Registration

Licensed Professional Engineer
State of _____ — No. 987654321, July, 19--

References

The best of references will be provided upon request.

SAMPLE RESUME
Engineering-Mechanical

FRANK M. DOE
Street
City, State, ZIP
(000) 000-0000

PROFESSIONAL OBJECTIVE

Seek a management position with an engineering-oriented firm where I can fully apply my education and experience.

EDUCATION

19___ 19___	Western State University City, State Bachelor of Science In Mechanical Engineering
19___	"Gating and Risering of Non-ferrous Materials" Seminar, Cast Metal Institute of America
19___	"Geometric Dimensional and Tolerancing for Quality Engineering" Seminar, Institute of Advance Technology
19___	"Basics Of Industrial Hydraulics" – Seminar, Management and Engineering Institute
19___	"Management Development For Engineers" – Symposium, The University Of The West - topics included managing maintenance systems and reliability, engineering, managing the manufacturing process, material science, starting-up new facilities and manufacturing for improved cost efficiency.

EXPERIENCE

19___ to present	American Foundry Corporation City, State Corporate Product Engineer Supervise engineering support for manufacturing hi-performance automotive wheels . . . develop manufacturing procedures for core room, molding, finishing and quality control . . . develop new programs for reducing scrap . . . develop gages and other instrumentation to control the quality of castings . . . implement gating changes to eliminate casting defects such as porosity and shrink.
19___ 19___	ABC Hardware Manufacturing Company City, State Industrial Engineer, Injection Molding - Analyzed and recommended manufacturing processes for a wide range of products

56

. . . calibrated Accufeeds and similar equipment . . . planned and developed molding, painting, inspection and final assembly procedures . . . participated on design team for new products.

19___   Automotive Foundry Division of ABC Industries
19___   City, State
Supervisor of Maintenance
Supervised 12 skilled trade employees . . . implemented machinery and scheduling improvement to reduce downtime . . . installed and tested new equipment . . . provided engineering support for plant management.

19___   Plant Engineer
19___   Planned, designed and implemented new systems to improve production and quality . . . provided on-going maintenance and inspection of hydraulic, pneumatic and other mechanical systems . . . assisted purchasing and plant management in establishing specifications for capital equipment . . . provided engineering services including drafting for allied plants.

19___   XYZ Construction Equipment Corporation
19___   City, State
Engineer
Assisted marketing personnel in developing product features for heavy construction equipment . . . tested all equipment prior to customer delivery . . . provided on-site technical assistance to customers.

SUMMARY OF QUALIFICATIONS

Possess solid experience in all aspects of mechanical engineering including planning, designing, developing manufacturing, trouble-shooting along with managing people, products and profits.

SPECIAL SKILLS

Speak, read and write fluent German . . . travelled extensively in Europe contacting leading vehicle manufactures . . . possess strong combination of technical and human relations skills.

REFERENCES

Available upon request.

Deborah R. Doe

Street
City, State, Zip
(000) 000-0000

Career Objective   To achieve a position of Manager of General Accounting where I can fully apply my education and experience.

Employment History

19— to present   Manager of Accounts Payable
ABC Enterprises, Incorporated
City, State

Presently supervise a staff of seven individuals. Verify and reconcile all orders with receiving documents and invoices. Ensure that all earned discounts are taken. Issue annual payments amounting to over $75 million.

19— to 19—   Supervisor, Accounts Receivable
General Manufacturing Corporation
City, State, Zip

Supervised five individuals. Monitored all receivables and maintained close control over past-due accounts. Provided financial department with daily reports listing all overdue accounts and the actions taken. Coordinated information on seriously overdue accounts with all internal departments.

19— to 19—   Accounting clerk
XYZ Company
City, State, Zip

Prepared monthly cost analysis reports for assigned products. Developed and recommended annual price increases on assigned products. Prepared price quotations on replacement products for the replacement market. Prepared original equipment prices for quotation to the vehicle manufacturers.

Education

19– to 19–	National University City, State B.B.A. with a major in accounting
19– to 19–	Southview High School City, State
June, 19–	"Managing The Accounts Payable Function" Seminar presented by National Accounting Institute
March, 19–	"Effective Computerization Of Accounts Receivables" Seminar presented by Smith, Hopkins and Jones
July, 19–	"Improving Your Cost Analysis" Seminar presented by National Association of Accounting

Significant Accomplishments

Developed computerized system for the accounts receivable department resulting in a 14% reduction in overdue accounts and a 17% decrease in non-collectibles. Prepared cost analysis of a mature product line which led to a new manufacturing process providing a 27% increase in profitability.

Memberships

National Association of Accountants
President of local chapter — 19–.

References

The best of references will be furnished upon request.

SAMPLE RESUME
Law

SANDRA A. DOE

Street
City, State, ZIP
(000) 000-0000

PROFESSIONAL OBJECTIVE

   I am seeking a challenging position offering career opportunities in labor and law.

EDUCATION

19___
19___   University of the East School of Law   Grade Average:
              City, State   3.87
              Juris Doctor
              Honors: Recipient of Horton Scholarship
                      Honors In Legal Writing
              Activities: U of E Legal Society

19___   State University   Grade Average:
              City, State   3.89
              Paralegal Certification

19___   University of New England   Grade Average:
              City, State   3.88
              Bachelor of Arts
              Major: Political Science
              Honors: Summa Cum Laude Graduate
                        Michael E. Doe Award For Highest Achievement
                           In The English Department
                        Presidential Award Recipient at Honors'
                           Conference
                        Dean's List
              Activities: National English Honor Society
                           Debating Society
                           Pre-Law Society; Social Science Club

EXPERIENCE

19___
19___   American Chemical Corporation
              City, State
              Personnel Legal Specialist
              Conducted research on State Worker's Compensation Law.
              Administered pre-employment testing program and other hiring
                 criteria.
              Prepared individual termination and early retirement plans.
              Assisted in Supervisory Training.

| 19___ | Lake County Community College |
| 19___ | City, State |

Instructor of Business Law

Taught basic contract, negotiable instruments, torts and civil procedure.

| 19___ | Monroe and Knopp |
| 19___ | City, State |

Summer Intern:

Administered residential and commercial real estate with strong customer contact.

Conducted research.

Prepared residential and commercial closings.

Prepared estate documents and various estate tax records.

Performed legal research.

Examined legal documents to ensure conformity to federal and state laws.

| 19___ | State House of Representatives |
| 19___ | City, State |

Drafted House and Senate Bills for Department of Labor.

Provided administrative support to State Personnel and Labor Departments.

MEMBERSHIPS

Financial City Law Society

State Legal Association

National Bar Association

REFERENCES

Available upon request.

SAMPLE RESUME
Manufacturing

John F. Doe
Street
City, State 00000
(000) 000-0000

POSITION OBJECTIVE

Production - Inventory Manager - Materials Control Manager

GENERAL SUMMARY

B.S. in Business Administration
M.A. in Industrial Management
Knowledge of Production Scheduling
Production and Inventory Control
Initiated Just-In-Time System
Coordinated Production Scheduling with Marketing Group
Supervised Personnel
Manufacturing Auditor

BUSINESS EXPERIENCE

ABC Manufacturing Company
City, State
19-- to 19--

PRODUCTION PLANNING MANAGER

Directed scheduling at (city) plant which employed 3,000 persons and manufactured approximately 3 million widgets a year.

Controlled finished goods and in-process production. Coordinated the production schedule of all products with the Sales and Marketing Research groups.

Scheduled employee work hours including overtime and recommended changes in the work force.

Established production schedules based on input from Marketing Research, industry sources and customer demand.

SUPERVISORY RESPONSIBILITIES

Supervised five production schedulers.

MAJOR ACCOMPLISHMENTS

Initiated a Just-In-Time Inventory Control System for reducing capital requirements.

Reduced in-house inventory by 27% during a two year period.

Coordinated the development of a Marketing Research-Production Plannying System involving 18,000 part numbers.

ASSISTANT PRODUCTION MANAGER

> XYZ CORPORATION
> City, State
> 19– to 19–

Assisted in directing all product scheduling and manufacturing operations. Participated in the development of a computerized inventory and production scheduling system.

MANUFACTURING TRAINEE

Participated in the training of personnel in virtually all manufacturing operations including inventory scheduling, quality control and auditing. Responsible for the scheduling of the _____ line for overseas shipments.

INTERNAL AUDITOR

Responsible for assisting in the auditing of all manufacturing operations. Conducted annual inventory analysis of the entire (city) plant.

EDUCATION

> American College
> City, State
> B.S. in Business Administration — 19–

> University of America
> City, State
> M.A. in Industrial Management — 19–

> "Production Scheduling" - A seminar presented by the American Manufacturing Association — 19–

> "Optimum Inventory Management" - A seminar presented by the National Inventory Management Association — 19–

> "Achieving Manufacturing Excellence" - A seminar presented by the University of USA — 19–

REFERENCES

The best of references will be furnished upon request.

SAMPLE RESUME
Mechandising

MARTIN M. DOE
Street
City, State, ZIP
(000) 000-0000

CAREER OBJECTIVE

To be a Merchandising Manager or Assistant Manager of a medium size organization.

EDUCATION

19___	Southern State University
19___	City, State
	Bachelor of Business Administration
	Major: Marketing
	Minor: Merchandising
19___	"Developing Effective Consumer Promotions" — National Management Association
19___	"Creating Successful Trade Promotions" — Seminar, Institute of Advertising and Merchandising

EMPLOYMENT

19___ to present	Gulf Shore Hardware Corporation
	City, State
	Merchandising Specialist
	Develop trade and consumer promotions including coupon and sweepstakes programs. Create and purchase point-of-purchase material, premiums and packaging. Design booths and displays for shows and exhibits. Coordinate merchandising programs in close cooperation with marketing personnel.
19___ 19___	American Marine Company
	City, State
	Sales Representative
	Sold a complete line of marine hardware to wholesalers and dealers. Represented the Company at marine trade shows throughout the south.
19___ 19___	Gulfport Marina
	City, State
	Manager
	Managed a marina with 42 slips. Responsible for store and fuel sales.

SIGNIFICANT ACCOMPLISHMENTS

Developed sweepstakes promotion in 19___ that attracted over 3 million entries. Developed pegboard display that was purchased by thousands of hardware stores and received recognition as one of the top 10 displays of the year by the National Packaging Association. Increased marine hardware sales in my region by 23% between 19___ and 19___.

SPECIAL SKILLS

Excel in both person-to-person and group presentations.

REFERENCES

Available upon request.

SAMPLE RESUME
Nursing

JOAN S. DOE
Street
City, State, Zip
(000) 000-0000

Professional Objective

To be a Nursing Supervisor in the cardiology department of a large Mid-Western Hospital.

Clinical Experiences

19-- to present   University Medical Center
                    Medical Plaza
                    City, State

                    Perform nursing duties for patients in 36 bed Cardiac Unit. Take histories, administer medications, maintain charts and prepare patients for tests, surgery and treatments.

19-- to 19--   St. Mary's Hospital
                    City, State

                    Performed general staff nursing duties

19-- to 19--   EKG Technician
                    Great Lakes Medical Foundation
                    City, State

19-- to 19--   Medical-Surgical Nursing
                    St. John Hospital
                    City, State

19-- to 19--   Physician's Medical Assistant
                    Robert R. Doe, M.D. Cardiologist
                    City, State

Education

19.. to 19..	University of America
	City, State
	B.S.N.
	Top 15% of Class
19..	University of America
	Medical Center
	City, State
	R.N.
	BLS Certification

Campus Activities

Student Professional Nurses 19.. to 19..
Health Center Volunteer 19.. to 19..

Major Accomplishments

Selected by University of America to discuss "Careers in Nursing" at area community colleges.

Appointed by Department of Cardiology Chairman to serve on the University Medical Center inter-disciplinary team for counseling seriously ill patients.

Memberships

Americn Nursing Association
———— State Nursing Association
Cardiac Nurses of America

References

The best of professional references will be furnised upon request.

ETHEL A. DOE

**Street
City, State, Zip
(000) 000-0000**

CAREER OBJECTIVE

To obtain a position as an occupational therapist in an acute/rehabilitation hospital where I can fully apply my skills in evaluating, planning, and implementing patient treatment.

EDUCATION

19___   Eastern Technical College
19___   Bachelor of Science in Occupational Therapy
          Registered Occupational Therapist

EDUCATIONAL EXPERIENCES

Adult Physical Dysfunction Level II
(four months) Jan. - April 19___
Saint Mary's Hospital
City, State
Duties included evaluation, planning and implementing treatment.

Adult Physical Dysfunction Level I
General Hospital
City, State
Fieldwork (one month) May, 19_____
Responsibilities included clinical observation, planning and implementing treatment. Diagnosed patients having neurological and musculoskeletal dysfunctions.

Pediatric Physical Dysfunction Level I
Fieldwork (one month) Sept., 19___
North Central University Hospital
City, State
Evaluated and treated children with various development abnormalities. Prepared extensive reports upon completion of each session.

Adult Psychosocial Dysfunction Level II
Fieldwork (three months) Oct., Nov., Dec. 19___
Forrest County Hospital
City, State
Evaluated and treated patients with major depression, schizophrenia and various personality disorders. Interviewed, identified problems and scheduled therapuetic activities to attain treatment objectives. Duties included activity analysis, case study presentations and comparative analysis of various treatment programs. Responsibilities also included group therapy treatments.

RELATED PROFESSIONAL EXPERIENCE

Metropolitan Clinic Hospital
City, State
Volunteer for providing non-nursing support to patients being treated for both physical and mental abnormalities.

HONORS

Member of American Honor Society

PROFESSIONAL MEMBERSHIPS

Student Occupational Therapy Club – selected to represent Club at the Tri-County Medical Council, State Occupational Association, National Association of Occupational Therapist

REFERENCES

Available upon request.

SAMPLE RESUME
Personnel

LISA S. DOE

Street
City, State
(000) 000-0000

PROFESSIONAL OBJECTIVE

I am seeking a position as Personnel Manager where I can fully apply my education and experience.

EDUCATION

19__	University of Mid-Town	Grade Average:
19__	City, State	3.8
	Bachelor of Business Administration	
	Major: Human Resources Management	
	Minor: Communications	

Activities: Business Club - Vice-President, Staff Editor for school newspaper, member of debating team

19__	University of the North	Grade Average:
19__	City, State	3.7
19__	Master of Arts in Human Resources	

Prepared thesis titled "Trends In Corporate Loyalty."

19__   "Improving Your Hiring Program" – Seminar, National Personnel Association.

19__   "Latest Developments In Employment Law" – Seminar, National Legal Advisors Association.

19__   "Computerizing Personnel Management" – Seminar, American Association of Human Resources Executives

EMPLOYMENT

19__
to
present

American Manufacturing Company
City, State
Assistant Personnel Manager
Responsible for assisting the Personnel Manager in all human resources functions for a work force of 700 hourly and salaried persons. Responsible for recruiting, screening, placing, evaluating and processing all separations and terminations. Responsible for implementing Affirmative Action Program and serve as E.E.O.C. Liason Coordinator.

19____ to 19____	**Midwest Paper Corporation** **City, State** **Personnel Specialist** Responsible for initial interviewing of prospective employees. Prepared all personnel forms and recruiting advertisements working closely with the legal department. Processed all evaluation forms and prepared rankings by various cost centers. Assisted in administrating the employee benefits program.
19____ 19____	**General Retailing Corporation** **City, State** **Personnel Trainee** Performed entry level functions in the personnel department. Maintained personnel files for 380 employees. Assisted in processing medical claims and other employee benefits. Assisted in preparing materials for supervisory development program.

SIGNIFICANT ACCOMPLISHMENTS

Developed employee orientation program which was adopted by my present employer at three other locations. Prepared and implemented new performance appraisal program which gained strong management support. Prepared article published in National Personnel Executive Magazine titled "The Critical role of Today's Performance Appraisal."

REFERENCES

The best of professional references will be provided upon request.

SAMPLE RESUME
Product Management

JAMES F. DOE

Street
City, State, Zip
(000) 000-0000

CAREER OBJECTIVE

To obtain a challenging position as Product Manager for a consumer goods manufacturer.

EDUCATION

19__	University of the North	Grade Average:
19__	City, State	3.7
	Master of Arts In Business	
	Major: Marketing	

19__	Lake College	Grade Average:
19__	City, State	3.6
	Bachelor of Business Administration	
	Major: Marketing	
	Minor: Communications	

RELATED EDUCATION

19__   "Managing The Product Management Function" — Seminar, National Management Association

19__   "Selling To Mass Marketers" — Seminar, American Institute of Sales

19__   "Improving Your Human Relations" — Seminar, Northern State University

EMPLOYMENT

19__
to
present

American Cosmetics, Inc.
Product Manager
Responsible for the success of the hair spray line including bottom-line profit . . . responsible for developing new products, planning marketing programs including advertising, merchandising, packaging and sales . . . maintain close coordination with the advertising agency, sales force, research and financial groups.

19__
19__

Ace Cosmetics, Inc.
City, State
Sales Representative – called on department stores and speciality shops promoting sales of the Ace cosmetic line.

SIGNIFICANT ACCOMPLISHMENTS

Developed a new hair spray travel line which reached multi-million dollar sales within two years . . . Increased sales in my district 21% between 19___ and 19___. Received Sales Person of the Year Award for 19___.

SPECIAL SKILLS

Possess strong communication and presentation skills . . . excel in human relations qualities.

MEMBERSHIPS

National Association of Product Managers – American Society of Sales Executives – Vice President of local chapter – 19___.

REFERENCES

Available upon request.

SAMPLE RESUME
Public Relations

JOSEPH R. DOE
Street
City, State, Zip
(000) 000 0000

CAREER OBJECTIVE

To be a Public Relations Manager for a medium to large size organization.

EDUCATION

19___	Eastern University	Grade Average:
19___	City, State	3.7
	Master of Arts in Journalism	

19___	Central State University	Grade Average:
19___	City, State	3.6
	Bachelor of Arts	
	Major: Communications	
	Minor: Political Science	

19___   "Managing The Public Relations Function" — Seminar, American Society of Public Relations Executives

19___   "Working Effectively With The Media" — Seminar, National Public Relations Association

EMPLOYMENT

19___
to
present
    XYZ Corporation
City, State
Promoted in June of 19___ to Assistant Public Relations Manager. Assist the Public Relations Manager in planning and implementing all department functions. Prepare articles promoting the Company's products. Prepare extensive new product announcements working closely with the departments of research, manufacturing and marketing. Prepare news releases and respond to all inquiries regarding the Company, its products and employees.

19___
19___
    Public Relations Trainee
Assisted in preparing news releases and the Company's Annual Report.
Wrote articles for the Company's house organ. Prepared quarterly news releases of earnings working in close coordination with the financial department. Responsible for managing the Company's plant tour program.

**SIGNIFICANT
ACCOMPLISHMENTS**

Wrote cover copy for the Company's 19___ Annual Report which won the Bronz Award For Excellence by the National Institute of Corporate Communications. Developed a plant tour program which was implemented at the Company's seven other domestic manufacturing facilities.

**SPECIAL
SKILLS**

Possess a strong knowledge of photography and graphics design.

ORGANIZATIONS

American Society of Public Relations Executives - Vice-President of Local Chapter, National Photographic Association

REFERENCES

Available upon request.

SAMPLE RESUME
Purchasing

RICHARD A. DOE   **Street**
                                                    City, State, Zip
                                                    (000) 000-0000

CAREER OBJECTIVE

Seek a position as Purchasing Manager for a medium to large size firm.

EDUCATION

Western State University
City, State
Bachelor of Business Administration
Major: Procurement
Minor: Economics

Related Education

19___	"Succeeding With Just-In-Time Inventory Management" — Seminar, National Association of Purchasing Agents
19___	"Purchasing From Overseas Suppliers" — Seminar, International Purchasing Association
19___	"Computerizing the Purchasing Function" — Seminar, National Management Association

EXPERIENCE

19___ to present	American Tool Manufacturing, Inc. City, State Assistant Purchasing Manager. Supervise two purchasing Agents . . . purchase materials for manufacturing, operations and maintenance . . . supervise inventory control . . . develop specifications and optimum ordering quantities.
19___ thru 19___	West Coast Telephone Company City, State Purchasing Agent Purchased electrical equipment and supplies for the long distance group . . . maintained inventory control . . . solicited price quotations from U.S. and foreign suppliers . . . toured supplier plants to inspect for quality control.

SIGNIFICANT ACCOMPLISHMENTS

Implemented computerized program for maintaining inventory control, optimum ordering points and prices . . . prepared a corporate purchasing policy statement . . . reduced inventory cost by 14% between 19___ and 19___

SPECIAL SKILLS

Excel in working effectively with all internal departments and vendors. Extremely quality conscious.

REFERENCES

The best of references will be furnished upon request.

SAMPLE RESUME
Sales

Susan M. Doe
Street
City, State, Zip
(000) 000-0000

Career Objective

Seek a sales or marketing position that requires a creative, productive and goal-oriented individual. Desire a company that provides strong challenges and offers long term career growth potential.

Work Experience

ABC Realty, Inc.   City, State
Sales Agent

As a licensed real estate agent, engaged in all aspects of marketing services associated with a residential sales office. Requires excellent organizational and communication skills.

ABC Clothiers   City, State
Sales Manager

Responsible for all duties associated with the successful operation of a retail clothing store, including scheduling employee work hours, reconciling cash receipts and setting up merchandising displays. Required effective managerial and creative skills.

ABC Department Store   City, State
Department Manager

Responsible for the smooth operation of a retail apparel department within a major speciality chain. Authorized display arrangements, developed work schedules and audited cash receipts. Served as consultant for teen fashion board which required professional skills in the apparel industry.

ABC Apparel   City, State
Sales Assistant/Cashier

As store assistant, responsible for opening and closing of facility and all other functions associated with the operation of a retail unit. Required strong sales and organizational skills.

Education

ABC Institute, City, State
Associate's Degree, Business Management/Fashion Mechandising

ABC Community College, City, State
Completed courses in business and marketing areas.

Community Activities and Interests

Participated in Annual (City) Museum of Arts Membership Drive

Patron of Annual (City) Handicap Society Fashion Show

Active Fund Raiser for the Women's Shelter of (City) "Splash for Cash" Drive

Enjoy softball, aerobics, reading, swimming and fashion consulting activities.

References

The best of references will be provided upon request.

SAMPLE RESUME
Sales Management

JAMES S. DOE
Street
City, State, Zip
(000) 000-0000

Career Objective

I am seeking a more challenging position as a sales manager or a position offering equivalent responsibility. I am eager to demonstrate my ability to produce greater sales on a national level.

Professional Experience

19-- to Present — ABC Management Company, City, State.

I am presently Assistant Sales Manager responsible for all automotive aftermarket sales in the Eastern U.S. In my present capacity, I supervise 40 sales persons who achieved over 100 million in annual sales during 19--. For the previous three months, sales of my accounts are up 7.2% compared to last year.

19-- to 19-- — DEF Management Company, City, State.

As Manager of National Accounts, I was responsible for sales of (products) to major accounts such as (name of accounts). I was responsible for adding distribution through (name of accounts or level of distribution) representing a total of 1470 outlets.

Significant Accomplishments

While serving in the position of Assistant Sales Manager, I planned and introduced a new line of (product) which achieved a market penetration of 17% within two years.

Education

19-- to 19-- USA University, City, State — B.B.A. with a major in marketing.

19-- to 19-- Maintown High School — Graduated in top third of class.

19-- "Improving Sales Management Leadership" — Seminar, National Management Association

19-- "Motivating The Sales Force" — Seminar, American Society of Sales Executives

19-- "Improving your Selling Skills" — Seminar, University of America

19-- "Building Sales Through National Accounts" — Seminar, American Institute of Sales

Memberships

American Society of Sales Executives.
President of (City) chapter — 19--.

National Marketing Association

References

The best of references will be furnished upon request.

MARY R. DOE

Street
City, State, Zip
(000) 000-0000

Career Objective

I am seeking a secretarial position offering greater responsibilities and challenges.

Employment History

19-- to present   ABC Manufacturing Company
City, State

Presently serve as secretary to the Advertising Manager and
Assistant Advertising Manager. I provide full secretarial support
utilizing a number of popular software programs (list). I am also
responsible for monitoring the department budget and preparing
a division newsletter.

19-- to 19--   XYZ Corporation
City, State

As a clerk-typist, I performed general clerical duties in the Merchandising Department. Duties included mail distribution, typing
and filing.

Significant Accomplishments

I recently prepared a new software program to help monitor the
department budget. The new program was adopted by other
departments throughout the division and reduced the need for
temporary help.

Education

19-- to 19--   Northwest Community College
City, State

Graduate of two year program in Secretarial Studies

19-- to 19--   Central High School
City, State

Graduated in top third of class

Memberships	National Association of Secretaries
Interests	Sailing, reading and traveling Volunteer — United Appeal Campaign

References

The best of references will be furnished upon request.

SAMPLE RESUME
Teaching

JANE A. DOE

Present Address
Street
City, State, Zip
(000) 000-0000

After June 10, 19--
Street
City, State, Zip
(000) 000-0000

Career Objective
To secure a teaching position in the field of mathematics.

Education
USA University, City, State
Bachelor of Science Degree in Education, June, 19--
Major: Applied Mathematics
Minor: Business Mathematics
GPA: 3.4/4.0
California Certification: Mathematics, grades 7-12

Teaching Experience
Westland High School, City, State
Student Teaching Spring 19--
* Taught courses in algebra and geometry
* Advisor to Science Club

Wood County School District, Wood County, State
Special Teaching 19-- to 19--
* Taught over 200 hours of special education
* Tutored disadvantaged children with math problems

Bloomfield Hills Country Club, City, State, Summers 19-- to 19--
Swimming Coach
* Taught swimming

Activities
Tri-County Elderly Assistance Program 19-- to 19--
* Assisted nursing home residents in balancing checking accounts, budgeting and income tax preparation

USA University 19-- to 19--
City, State
* Undergraduate counselor

Social Sorority 19-- Present
* Treasurer
* Social Director
* Rush Committee

Other **Experiences**	Part-Time During College * Counter Person, ABC Copying Co. City, State * Cashier, Blue Ribbon Steak House, City, State Summers * Ride Operator, Blue Ridge Amusement Park, City, State * Waitress, Wood Hills Resort, City, State
Interests	Reading, swimming and tennis
References	The best of references will be furnished upon request.

SAMPLE RESUME
Writing

KAREN L. DOE
Street
City, State, Zip
(000) 000-0000

PROFESSIONAL OBJECTIVE

To obtain a position as a staff writer or editor for a magazine, newspaper or other publisher.

EDUCATION

State University   Grade Average:
City, State   3.8
Master of Arts in Journalism to be awarded in June, 19___

Great Northern University   Grade Average:
City, State   3.7
Bachelor of Arts
Major: Communications
Minor: English
Activities: Journalism Club - President
            Editor, School Newspaper 19___.
            American Journalism Society

"How To Effectively Report On Governmental Meetings And Hearings" — Seminar, National Association Of Newspaper Reporters, 19___.

EXPERIENCE

19___
to
present

Tri-County Publishing, Inc.
City, State
Part-time Staff Writer

Prepare articles and cover events as assigned by the editor. Attend and prepare summaries of county, city and township meetings. Attend school board meetings and prepare summaries for publication. Write special reports covering such subjects as environmental concerns, drug usage and crime. Maintain liaison with contributing reporters in many small towns.

SPECIAL SKILLS

Excellent writing skills with a strong ability to meet deadlines. Knowledge of environmental legislation, concerns and practices. Skilled photographer.

AWARDS

Recipient of 19___ State Journalism Society for series of articles on refuse collection.

**REFERENCES
AND PORTFOLIO**

The best of references and an extensive portfolio will be furnished upon request.

SAMPLE RESUME
Person Returning To Work Force

<u>Linda M. Doe</u>
Street
City, State, Zip
(000) 000-0000

<u>Career</u> <u>Objective</u>

I am eager to return to the educational field as a full time elementary teacher. My training and experience will enable me to make an important contribution to the education of the community's youth.

<u>Employment</u> <u>History</u>

19-- to 19--	Pine Street Elementary School City, State
	Taught third grade Named Elementary Teacher of the Year for 19--
19-- to 19--	Substitute Teacher Board of Education City, State

<u>Education</u>

19-- to 19--	USA University City, State Masters of Education
19-- to 19--	Mid-Western University City, State Bachelor of Education
<u>Memberships</u>	State Education Association. National Education Association Garden Club, Sorority Alumni Advisor
<u>Current</u> <u>Activities</u>	Right to Read Volunteer General Hospital Volunteer United Appeal Group Leader

<u>References</u>

The best of references will be furnished upon request.

SAMPLE RESUME
Part-Time

DAVID E. DOE
Street
City, State, Zip
(000) 000-0000

DESIRED POSITION

Laboratory Technician (part time)

EDUCATION

Medical College of USA
City, State
Presently a third year medical student

The USA University, B.S. 19--
City, State
Major-Biochemistry

RELEVANT COLLEGE COURSES

Subject	Total Quarter Hours
General Biology	15
Microbiology	5
Chemistry	32
Biochemistry	25
Physics	15

Hometown High School
City, State
Top 10% of class
Varsity football - 3 years

RELEVANT JOB EXPERIENCE

June 19-- to
September 19--

General Hospital
City, State
Volunteer - Serology and Hematology
   Laboratory
Assisted in conducting a wide range of
   blood tests

September, 19--
to June 19--

USA University
City, State
Chemistry laboratory instructor/teaching
   assistant

Summers of 19--   Worthington Animal Hospital City, State
thru 19--   Assisted in the care and treatment of animals

MEMBERSHIPS

American Society of Chemists

REFERENCES

The best of references will be provided upon request.

SAMPLE RESUME
Summer Job

Robert R. Doe
Street
City, State, Zip
(000) 000-0000

JOB OBJECTIVE

I am seeking a summer job where I can apply my interest in working with (the public, the land, children etc.)

EMPLOYMENT HISTORY

| 19-- to 19-- | Delivered newspapers |
| Summers of 19-- to 19-- | ABC Landscaping City, State |

EDUCATION

| 19-- to present | Central High School Member of band and staff Editor of yearbook |

STRENGTHS

I am ambitious, reliable and work well with others.

INTERESTS

Tennis and umpire for Little League

REFERENCES

The best of references will be furnished upon request.

XIV

Work Sheets

The following work sheets will enable you to draft your resume using different approaches. After completing your drafts, we suggest that you set them aside for later review.

A resume maintenance work sheet is included for recording activities that you will want to enter in future resumes. We recommend that you list new duties, special projects, additional training and significant achievements.

The resume status report provides a means to monitor your job hunting efforts. A methodical tracking system is essential to your success.

RESUME
Work Sheet

Functional Format

Name
Street
City, State, Zip
(000) 000-0000

CAREER OBJECTIVE

EXPERIENCE

Function

Function

Function

EMPLOYMENT HISTORY

EDUCATION

SIGNIFICANT ACCOMPLISHMENTS

REFERENCES

Functional Format

Name
Street
City, State, Zip
(000) 000-0000

CAREER OBJECTIVE

EXPERIENCE

Function

Function

Function

EMPLOYMENT HISTORY

EDUCATION

SIGNIFICANT ACCOMPLISHMENTS

REFERENCES

RESUME
Work Sheet

Chronological Format

Name
Street
City, State, Zip
(000) 000-0000

CAREER OBJECTIVE

EXPERIENCE

Function

Function

Function

EMPLOYMENT HISTORY

EDUCATION

SIGNIFICANT ACCOMPLISHMENTS

REFERENCES

RESUME MAINTENANCE
Work Sheet

**DATE   RESPONSIBILITIES, FUNCTIONS,
SIGNIFICANT ACCOMPLISHMENTS AND
OTHER CHANGES TO BE ADDED**

RESUME
Status Report

DATE	RESUME SENT TO	REJECTION LETTER REC.	FOLLOW-UP INQUIRY SENT	DATE OF INTERVIEW	INTERVIEW LETTER SENT	STATUS

Index

About the Author

James E. Neal Jr. has served in management capacities with a major multi-national firm. He is a graduate of the University of Toledo and the Institute of Labor and Industrial Relations of the University of Illinois. Mr. Neal is the President of Neal Publications, Inc. which he founded in 1978. He is the author of several widely acclaimed books in the field of human resources.

Notes

Notes

Notes